Famous Myths and Legends of the World

Myths and Legends of

ANCIENT ROME

WORLD
BOOK

a Scott Fetzer company
Chicago
www.worldbook.com

World Book, Inc.
180 North LaSalle Street
Suite 900
Chicago, Illinois 60601
USA

For information about other World Book publications, visit our website at **www.worldbook.com** or call **1-800-967-5325**.

Library of Congress Cataloging-in-Publication Data

Myths and legends of ancient Rome.
    pages cm. -- (Famous myths and legends of the world)
  Summary: "Myths and legends from Ancient Rome. Features include information about the history and culture behind the myths, pronunciations, lists of deities, word glossary, further information, and index"-- Provided by publisher.
  Includes index.
  ISBN 978-0-7166-2635-0
  1. Mythology, Roman--Juvenile literature. 2. Gods, Roman--Juvenile literature. 3. Rome--Folklore--Juvenile literature.
I. World Book, Inc. II. Series: Famous myths and legends of the world.
  BL803.M98 2015
  398.2'0937--dc23
                                        2015014766

Set ISBN: 978-0-7166-2625-1
E-book ISBN: 978-0-7166-2647-3 (EPUB3)

Printed in China by PrintWORKS Global Services, Shenzhen, Guangdong
2nd printing May 2016

Writer: Anita Croy

Staff for World Book, Inc.
Executive Committee
President: Jim O'Rourke
Vice President and Editor in Chief: Paul A. Kobasa
Vice President, Finance: Donald D. Keller
Vice President, Marketing: Jean Lin
Director, International Sales: Kristin Norell
Director, Human Resources: Bev Ecker

Digital
Director of Digital Products Development: Erika Meller
Digital Products Coordinator: Matthew Werner

Editorial
Manager, Annuals/Series Nonfiction: Christine Sullivan
Managing Editor, Annuals/Series Nonfiction:
    Barbara Mayes
Administrative Assistant: Ethel Matthews
Manager, Indexing Services: David Pofelski
Manager, Contracts & Compliance
    (Rights & Permissions): Loranne K. Shields

Manufacturing/Production
Manufacturing Manager: Sandra Johnson
Production/Technology Manager: Anne Fritzinger
Proofreader: Nathalie Strassheim

Graphics and Design
Senior Art Director: Tom Evans
Coordinator, Design Development and Production:
    Brenda Tropinski
Senior Designers: Matthew Carrington,
    Isaiah W. Sheppard, Jr.
Media Researcher: Rosalia Calderone
Manager, Cartographic Services: Wayne K. Pichler
Senior Cartographer: John M. Rejba

Staff for Brown Bear Books Ltd
Managing Editor: Tim Cooke
Editorial Director: Lindsey Lowe
Children's Publisher: Anne O'Daly
Design Manager: Keith Davis
Designer: Mike Davis
Picture Manager: Sophie Mortimer

CONTENTS

Diana, the goddess of the hunt, aims her bow at a deer, in a Roman mosaic from the A.D. 200's found in the modern country of Tunisia.

De Agostini Picture Library/ G. Dagli Orti/Bridgeman Images

Note to Readers:

Phonetic pronunciations have been inserted into the myths and legends in this volume to make reading the stories easier and to give the reader some of the flavor of the ancient Roman culture the stories represent. See page 64 for a pronunciation key.

The myths and legends retold in this volume are written in a creative way to provide an engaging reading experience and approximate the artistry of the originals. Many of these stories were not written down but were recited by storytellers from generation to generation. Even when some of the stories came to be written down they likely did not feature phonetic pronunciations for challenging names and words! We hope the inclusion of this material will improve rather than distract from your experience of the stories.

Some of the figures mentioned in the myths and legends in this volume are described on page 60 in the section "Deities of Ancient Rome." In addition, some unusual words in the text are defined in the Glossary on page 62.

INTRODUCTION

Since the earliest times, people have told stories to try to explain the world in which they lived. These stories are known as myths. Myths try to answer such questions as: How was the world created? Who were the first people? Where did the animals come from? Why does the sun rise and set? Why is the land devastated by storms or drought? Today, people often rely on science to answer many of these questions. But in earlier times—and in some parts of the world today—people explained natural events using stories about gods, goddesses, nature spirits, and heroes.

The World of Jupiter, Juno, and Io, page 24

Myths are different from folk tales and legends. Folk tales are fictional stories about animals or human beings. Most of these tales are not set in any particular time or place, and they begin and end in a certain way. For example, many English folk tales begin with the phrase "Once upon a time" and end with "They lived happily ever after." Legends are set in the real world, in the present or the historical past. Legends distort the truth, but they are based on real people or events.

Myths, in contrast, typically tell of events that have taken place in the remote past. Unlike legends, myths have also played—and often continue to play—an important role in a society's religious life. Although legends may have religious themes, most are not religious in nature. The people of a society may tell folk tales and legends for amusement, without believing them. But they usually consider their myths sacred and completely true. Most myths concern *divinities* or *deities* (divine beings).

These divinities have powers far greater than those of any human being. At the same time, however, many gods, goddesses, and heroes of mythology have human characteristics. They are guided by such emotions as love and jealousy, and they may experience birth and death. Mythological figures may even look like human beings. Often, the human qualities of the divinities reflect a society's ideals. Good gods and goddesses have the qualities a society admires, and evil ones have the qualities it dislikes. In myths, the actions of these divinities influence the world of humans for better or for worse.

The World of Apollo and Daphne, page 42

Myths can sometimes seem very strange. They sometimes seem to take place in a world that is both like our world and unlike it. Time can go backward and forward, so it is sometimes difficult to tell in what order events happen. People may be dead and alive at the same time.

Myths were originally passed down from generation to generation by word of mouth. Partly for this reason, there are often different versions of the same story. Many myths across cultures share similar themes, such as a battle between good and evil. But the myths of a society generally reflect the landscape, climate, and society in which the storytellers lived. Myths tell people about their distant history. They show people how to behave in the world and find their way. As teaching tools, myths help to prepare children for adulthood.

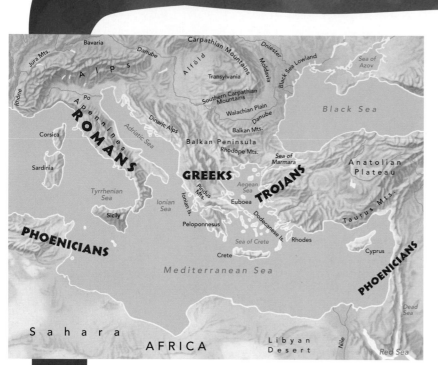

Myths and Legends of Ancient Rome

On the surface, the mythology of ancient Rome seems almost identical to that of ancient Greece. Strong similarities between Greek and Roman mythologies may come from the two cultures similar experiences of the southern European region and the Mediterranean Sea.

Before the Romans came into contact with Greek culture during the 700's B.C., they had developed their own mythology. They worshiped three major gods—Jupiter, Mars, and Quirinus (kwih RY nuhs). Jupiter ruled the heavens. Mars was the god of war. Quirinus seems to have represented the common people.

After the Romans came into contact with Greek culture, some Roman divinities began to reflect the qualities of Greek gods and goddesses. By the late 500's B.C., Jupiter, Juno, and Minerva had become the most important Roman gods. Jupiter remained the Romans' chief god. The Romans identified Juno with the Greek goddess Hera, the queen of the gods, and Minerva with Athena, the goddess of wisdom. Then between the 500's and 100's B.C., additional Roman mythological figures appeared, nearly all based on Greek divinities. Among these were Diana

(Artemis), Mercury (Hermes), Neptune (Poseidon), Pluto (Hades), Venus (Aphrodite), and Vulcan (Hephaestus). The Romans were a highly literate people. Many of their myths were written down in the Latin language relatively early in Roman history, even though the originals may have been told in the Greek world hundreds of years earlier.

In their mythology, the Romans—unlike the Greeks—tried to explain the founding and history of their nation. The Romans came to consider their divinities as historical figures. The best example of this historical emphasis is the story of Romulus and Remus, the mythical founders of Rome, supposedly in 753 B.C. During the 200's B.C., the Romans tried to relate the origins of their divinities to Greek myths. At this time, the Roman poet Virgil wrote an epic poem called the *Aeneid* in which he connected the origins of Rome to the events that followed the destruction of the city of Troy by the Greeks. He did this through the story of Aeneas, a Trojan prince, who was cast as the ancestor of Romulus and Remus.

The World of
Diana and Actaeon,
page 36

By studying myths, we can learn how different societies have answered basic questions about the world and the individual's place in it. By examining myths, we can better understand the feelings and values that bind members of society into one group. We can also compare the myths of various cultures to discover how these cultures differ and how they resemble one another.

AENEAS
and the Founding of Rome

The founding of Rome had its roots in the destruction of another mighty ancient city—Troy, on the coast of what is now Turkey.

One day Venus, the goddess of love, decided to pay a visit to Earth. She appeared in the splendid city of Troy. There she fell in love with a handsome Trojan prince named Anchises (an KY seez). Sometime later, Venus gave birth to a son, whom she and Anchises named Aeneas (ih NEE uhs).

For the first five years of his life, Aeneas was raised by the beautiful women who protected nature—the nymphs (nihmfs). Then Venus gave the boy to Anchises. The prince was so happy to have his son by his side that he unwisely told everyone that Aeneas's mother was the goddess Venus. When Jupiter, the king of the gods, heard Anchises's boasting, he was furious. Mere mortal men were forbidden to love goddesses! Jupiter flung a thunderbolt at Anchises, which hit him on the leg, leaving him lame.

Aeneas grew into a strong, fine-looking young man. He was a fearless warrior and a natural leader of people. But Aeneas was not destined to live in peace. A dispute between Troy and a land called Greece flared into a great war. For 10 years, Greek warriors besieged Troy. Finally, the Greeks captured the city, killed many of its people, and set it on fire.

Aeneas rescued his aged father and young son from Troy and escaped to nearby Mount Ida. Unhappily, Aeneas's wife was lost in the confusion. For months, Aeneas and other Trojan survivors built ships so they could search for a new home.

Finally, Aeneas left his homeland with a fleet of 20 ships. The fleet sailed from island to island across the Mediterranean

Sea. On one island, a fortuneteller told Aeneas that he would find his true home only when he became so hungry that he ate not only his food but also the plate it was served on. Aeneas sailed on, seeing marvelous lands and doing amazing things along the way.

At the powerful city of Carthage (KAHR thihj), Aeneas met its queen, Dido (DY doh), who fell desperately in love with him. Although Aeneas loved her, too, his duty to find a new home for his people forced him to leave Carthage. In despair, Dido threw herself from a cliff to her death. After many years at sea, Aeneas and his people reached the island of Sicily. There his father died. A heartbroken Aeneas buried his father and continued his journey.

Finally, Aeneas reached a land called Latium (LAY shee uhm). The people there were known as Latins (LAT uhnz). On his arrival, Aeneas left his people and journeyed to the underworld, where the dead remain for all time. There he learned about the people who would be

his descendants, the Romans, and the future glory of the city of Rome.

After Aeneas returned from the underworld, he and his fellow Trojans sat down along the banks of the River Tiber—where Rome would later stand—to share a meal. They were so famished that they ate not only the food but also the thin loaves of bread they were using as plates. The fortuneteller's prediction had come true! Aeneas had, indeed, found a new home for his people.

The king of Latium was named Latinus (luh TY nuhs). An oracle had once told him that a man from far away would marry his daughter, Lavinia (luh VIHN ee uh). Aeneas and King Latinus met, and the king offered to give Aeneas land for his people and Lavinia for his wife. The two men became allies and came to an agreement. Aeneas agreed that his people would call themselves Latins and speak the Latin language. In return, Latinus agreed that his people would worship the Trojans' gods.

Aeneas and Lavinia had a son named Silvius (SIHL vee uhs). Many generations later, a descendant of Aeneas and Lavinia would become the mother of Romulus (ROM yuh luhs) and Remus (REE muhs), the founders of Rome.

The World of **AENEAS**

The ancient Romans believed they were descended from Aeneas (ih NEE uhs), a warrior from the city of Troy. An ancient city in Asia Minor (now part of Turkey), Troy was made famous as the site of a great war in the legends of early Greece. Being descended from a Trojan hero gave the ancient Romans a heritage and a sense of continuity with a glorious past.

The Roman poet Virgil (70–19 B.C.) made Aeneas the hero of an epic poem called the *Aeneid* (ih NEE ihd). Written in 12 parts between 30 and 19 B.C., the *Aeneid* tells the story of Aeneas's journey from Troy to Rome. The *Aeneid,* which was modeled on Homer's famous Greek epic poem, the *Odyssey*, is the national epic of ancient Rome.

According to myth, Aeneas disappeared from this world during a battle with a neighboring people called the Etruscans. In some versions of the myth, he was taken to heaven and became a god.

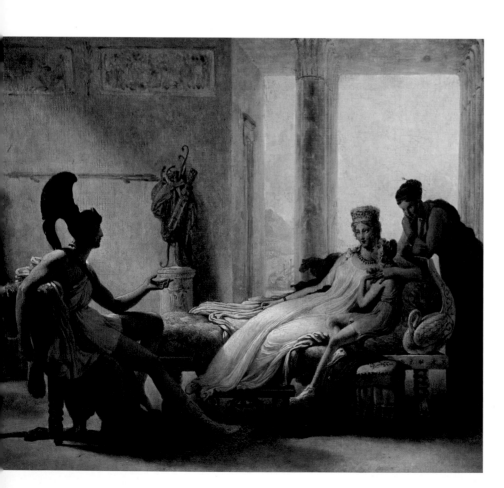

Aeneas tells Dido (DY doh), the founder and queen of Carthage (KAHR thihj), the story of his escape from Troy and journey across the Mediterranean Sea, in a painting from 1815. Ancient Carthage, a once-wealthy city in northern Africa, near the modern-day city of Tunis, Tunisia, was destroyed by Rome in the mid-140's B.C., during the third war fought between the two powers.

THE RIVER TIBER

The city of Rome was founded on seven wooded hills next to the Tiber (TY buhr) River, one of the longest rivers in Italy. As Rome grew, the city expanded into the swampy lowlands beneath the hills. These parts of Rome often suffered damaging floods from the Tiber. But the Tiber also provided a convenient route to the Tyrrhenian Sea—a part of the Mediterranean Sea—which lies about 15 miles (24 kilometers) to the west. The harbor at Ostia, a town at the mouth of the Tiber, allowed for extensive trade with other communities.

Jupiter, the king of the gods and ruler of the universe in ancient Rome, used a thunderbolt as a weapon. Jupiter was originally the god of the sky and of such weather events as thunder and lightning.

ROMULUS

The story of the founding of Rome is a bloody tale of twin brothers who were hungry for power.

King Numitor (NOO mih tohr) was the rightful ruler of the Latins. But his ambitious brother, Amulius (uh MYOO ee uhs), was determined to seize the throne. He overthrew Numitor and killed Numitor's two sons so they could not grow up and avenge their father.

Then Amulius ordered Rhea Silvia (REE uh SIHL vee uh), Numitor's daughter, to become a Vestal Virgin. He knew that these priestesses were required by law to remain untouched by men. In this way, Amulius hoped that Rhea Silvia would never have children who might threaten his rule.

But even though she was a Vestal Virgin, Rhea Silvia had no power to resist a god. Mars, the god of war, seduced her, and she gave birth to twin boys. When Amulius found out, he was furious. He killed Rhea Silvia and ordered the babies

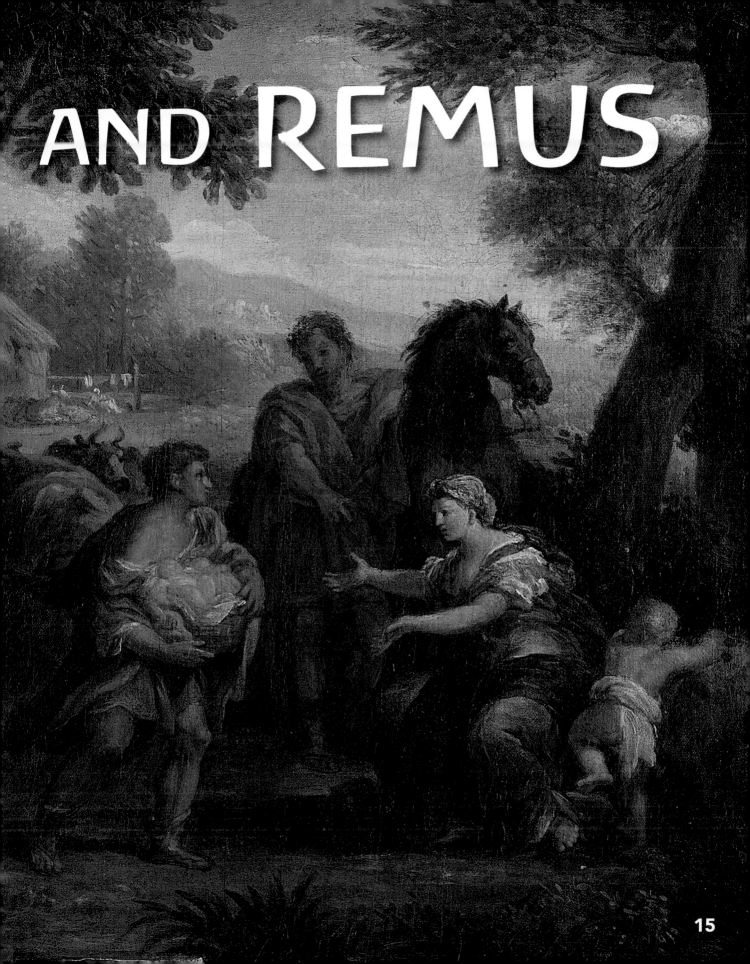

AND REMUS

to be drowned in the River Tiber. But his servants could not bring themselves to kill the boys. Instead, they set them adrift on the water.

Even so, the boys probably would have drowned if Mars had not acted. Mars made sure the babies floated to the riverbank. Then he sent a she-wolf to feed the boys with milk from her breast and a woodpecker to give them bits of food. Eventually, the boys were found by a shepherd named Faustulus (FOWST yuh luhs). Faustulus was actually Amulius's chief shepherd, and he knew that if the king discovered that he had rescued the boys, he would be killed. But Faustulus protected the boys anyway and named them Romulus (ROM yuh luhs) and Remus (REE muhs).

Romulus and Remus grew into strong, healthy boys who were brave and smart. One day, Faustulus decided it was time to tell the boys that they were not the sons of a shepherd but heirs to the throne of the Latins. Furious at the news, they rushed to see their grandfather Numitor. Between them, they devised a plan to overthrow Amulius. With the help of their shepherd friends and those men who still supported Numitor, they organized a rebellion. Amulius was killed and Numitor restored to his throne.

But the twins did not want to wait to inherit the throne from their grandfather. They decided to found their own city and choose a spot close to the River Tiber, where they had been rescued. But that was the only thing they could agree on. They could not decide which one of them would be the ruler, what they would call their city, or any other detail. The twins did not know which of them was the older, so they could not even use that as a means of settling their disagreement. Finally, they agreed that the twin who saw the largest number of vultures in flight would make the choices.

Romulus and Remus went to the top of a hill. There Remus saw 6 vultures; Romulus saw 12 vultures. Each declared that he had fulfilled the omen: Remus saw the vultures first, but Romulus had seen more vultures. Unable to agree, the twins started to fight. During the heated argument, Romulus killed his brother.

Now alone, Romulus built a city on the hill where his brother had fallen. He called the new city Rome, after himself. Later, the Romans would call the place the Palatine Hill.

The World of ROMULUS AND REMUS

According to legend, Rome was founded in 753 B.C. Originally a small farming community, Rome became the center of one of the greatest empires in history.

THE HILLS OF ROME

The city of Rome was founded on seven wooded, flat-topped hills. The hills offered good protection from enemy attack. The steep Palatine Hill and the even steeper Capitoline (KAP uh tuh lyn) Hill lay at the heart of the city. The other hills were the Aventine, the Caelian (SEE lee uhn), the Esquiline (EHS kwuh lyn), the Quirinal (KWIHR uh nuhl), and the Viminal (VIHM uh nuhl). Today, the city stretches over about 20 hills.

Roman soldiers were among the most important members of Roman society, and Mars, the god of war, was one of the most important gods. The Romans expanded their empire through conquest. They believed that their gods rewarded their devotion to them with military victories.

Priestesses called Vestal Virgins offer a sacrifice to Vesta, the goddess of the hearth, at her temple in the Forum of Rome, the center of government. In the temple, a sacred flame burned day and night, symbolizing the Roman belief in the eternity of the city. Seven Vestal Virgins tended the flame and performed such symbolic household duties for the state as making sacred cakes for the festivals of Rome's gods. Being chosen as a Vestal Virgin was a great honor, and the priestesses had power and public respect and were well guarded. In exchange, they had to promise not to marry for 30 years. Those who broke this promise were buried alive.

THE ETRUSCANS

For 150 years, from the 500's to the 400's B.C., the Etruscans (ih TRUHS kuhnz) controlled Rome. The Etruscans were originally from Lydia, an ancient country in what is now Turkey. Although Etruscan culture was more advanced than that of the early Romans, modern researchers know relatively little about them, mainly because Etruscan writing has not been completely *deciphered* (translated into a modern language). About 13,000 written specimens remain of the Etruscan language, which was written in a script much like ancient Greek. Although modern scholars can interpret individual words and phrases, they cannot fully understand the language. The Etruscans introduced the foundations of Roman culture, including the Senate (a governing and lawmaking group), expansion through war, and the cult of priests.

The Etruscan Arch was one of seven entrances to the ancient city of Perugia, a major Etruscan city in Italy. Built in the 200's B.C., the arch was restored in 40 B.C. by the Romans after they conquered Perugia.

JUPITER, JUNO, AND IO

Jupiter, the king of the gods, had many relationships with goddesses and human women. Such encounters usually ended badly for those who caught his eye.

One day, the goddess Juno (JOO noh), the jealous wife of Jupiter (JOO puh tuhr), the king of the gods, grew suspicious. The sky had suddenly gone dark as a cloud covered the sun. Juno wondered if Jupiter had made the cloud to hide something. When she blew the cloud away, she saw Jupiter sitting on the bank of a river next to a cow.

Knowing her husband as she did, Juno suspected that the cow might be something—or someone—other than a big field animal. In fact, the cow was really the nymph Io (EYE oh), the beautiful daughter of the river god Inachus (IHN uh kus). Jupiter had been flirting with Io, and when Juno had appeared, he had changed Io into a cow.

Juno approached her husband and asked him about the cow. She admired the cow and asked her husband if she might have the cow as a gift. What was Jupiter to do? If he refused to give the cow to his wife, she would know that he had been flirting. But if he gave Io to Juno, what would happen to the lovely river nymph?

Jupiter realized he had no choice but to give the cow to Juno. As Juno was leading the cow away, she cast a spell on Io so she would remain a cow forever. Then Juno told her devoted servant Argus (AHR guhs) to keep guard over it. Now, Argus had 100 eyes, only half of which closed at one time in sleep. This meant he could watch Io constantly.

Poor Io, trapped inside the cow's body, could not escape. She could not call out for help because she was a cow. Her family became worried about her disappearance and looked everywhere for her. But they did not think that the cow, with its shiny hide, was really Io. They admired the cow, patting her back. Io licked her father's outstretched hand, but he did not know it was his daughter.

Realizing that he had to save Io, Jupiter called his son Mercury, the messenger god, to help him. He told Mercury to make Argus fall asleep. So Mercury pretended to be a shepherd watching his flock. As he strolled around, he played on his pipes. Argus had never heard such lovely music and called over to Mercury, "Young man, come and sit by me in the shade. You can watch your sheep and play your pipes." Mercury did as he was asked and played soothing music. Before long, Argus's eyes began to close in sleep until all 100 were shut. Then Mercury quickly cut off Argus's head with one sweep of his sword.

Juno was furious. She took Argus's eyes and put them into the tail of the peacock, where they remain to this day. To punish Jupiter and Io, Juno sent a biting, bloodsucking fly to torment the cow. Io fled across the world, desperately trying to shake off the fly, but she could not escape from it. Finally, Jupiter told Juno that he would not spend any more time with Io if Juno would restore the nymph. Juno agreed and turned Io back into a nymph. Io went back to her family and lived happily.

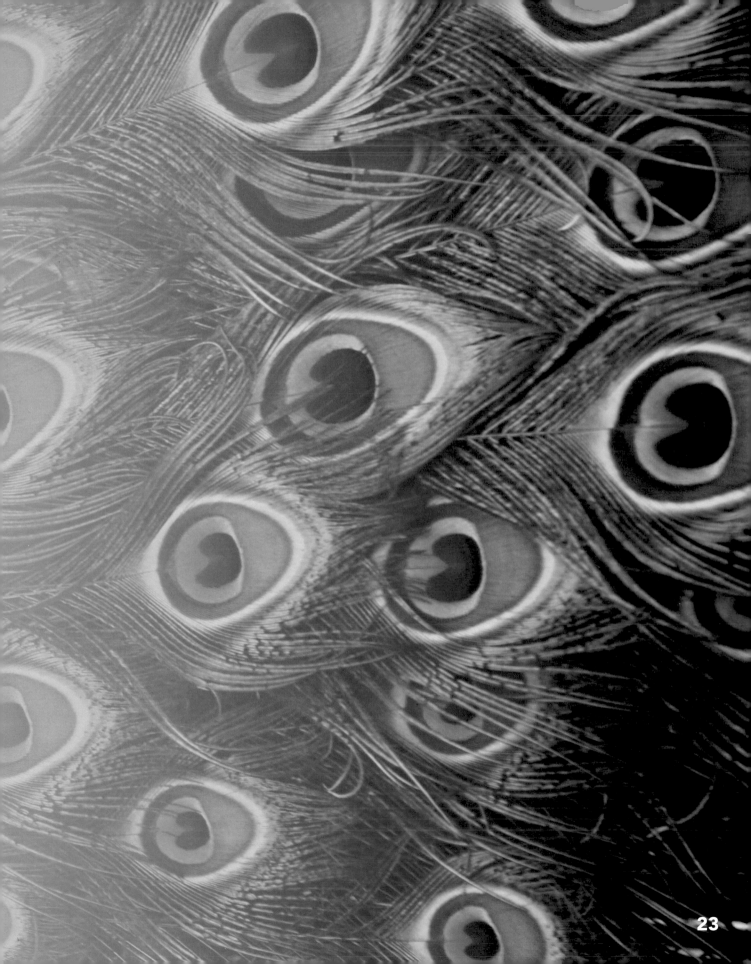

The World of
JUPITER, JUNO, AND IO

Jupiter (JOO puh tuhr), the king of the gods in Roman mythology, was married to Juno (JOO noh), the queen of the gods. Jupiter had many lovers, including goddesses, nymphs, and human women. Juno was often jealous and did cruel things to Jupiter's lovers.

JUNO

Juno, Jupiter's wife, was also a powerful divinity in her own right. Romans believed that she was the goddess of the sacred institution of marriage and that she looked after women during childbirth. Many Roman myths tell of Juno becoming angry with her husband for his constant love affairs and the harsh punishments she inflicted on the women and nymphs involved. The peacock, mentioned in "Jupiter, Juno, and Io," was one of the symbols of Juno.

Ancient Romans called on Janus (JAY nuhs), the two-faced god of beginnings, at the start of every prayer, even ahead of Jupiter. Janus had one face looking toward the future and one looking toward the past. (The month of January, the first month of the year in the Western calendar, is named for Janus.) Janus is often shown holding a key to symbolize his power as the god of gates and doors and of entrances and exits.

Ancient Romans also prayed to Janus at the start and finish of all important actions, especially war. During wartime, the temple of Janus in Rome was left open to show that Janus had gone to help the Romans on the battlefield. Once peace was declared, the doors were closed again.

Jupiter, also called Jove (johv), was the most revered of all the Roman gods because, as the sky god, he had the power to send Earth fair weather or destructive storms. He caused rain to fall, enabling crops to grow. He was also the god of thunder and lightning and other atmospheric events. Jupiter used a thunderbolt as a weapon. Jupiter also made certain that mortals lived out their lives according to their fate.

As Roman society developed, Jupiter became the god of laws and truth. Myths told how he handed out stiff punishments to those who committed crimes. He was the god before whom most *oaths* (promises) were sworn. By the middle of the 200's B.C., Jupiter's influence had grown and he had become the main protector of Rome. He was also called Jupiter Optimus Maximus ("The Best and Greatest").

CERES AND PERSEPHONE

Despite the pleas of the goddess Ceres, not even Jupiter himself could wholly free their daughter, Persephone, from the underworld.

Persephone (puhr SEHF uh nee) was the beautiful daughter of Ceres (SIHR eez), the goddess of the fields, orchards, and fruitful harvests, and Jupiter (JOO puh tuhr), the king of the gods. It is thanks to Ceres's good will that the grain and the fruit and vegetables grow each year. For this reason, the people honored Ceres with sacrifices and festivals. The people knew that if Ceres grew sad or angry, the crops might not grow. The thing that made Ceres the happiest was spending time with her beloved daughter, Persephone.

One day, under the shining and warm sun, Persephone was picking colorful flowers in a field. She did not see Pluto (PLOO toh), the fearsome god of Hades (HAY deez), the underworld, and her uncle, approach in his ghostly chariot.

Pluto was dazzled by the beauty of his niece Persephone and overcome by a powerful desire to make her his queen in the world of the dead. He drove his chariot upon Persephone and snatched her from the field of flowers before any of her companions could warn her or stop Pluto. Pluto took Persephone to one of the darkest and deepest corners of his grim kingdom.

When Ceres discovered that her daughter was missing, she was heartbroken. She refused to fulfill any of her duties as an Earth goddess until Persephone was returned to her.

Meanwhile, Pluto had imprisoned Persephone in a cave deep within the underworld. She wept and wept and refused to speak to Pluto. He offered

her many kinds of delicious food, but she refused it all. She knew the story that if you ate anything that Pluto gave you, you would never leave the underworld. She had no idea if the story was true, but she certainly did not want to risk being trapped in the underworld with Pluto forever.

For a week, Persephone did not allow a single morsel to pass her lips. Finally, she became so hungry that she ate six pomegranate seeds, thinking that they would not really count. But they did. Her fate was sealed. From then on, Persephone was condemned to live in the underworld.

Jupiter, who was watching over Earth, grew more and more worried. The crops were failing because Ceres was too upset to tend to them. Jupiter realized that people would die if there was no harvest. So he sent his son Mercury, the

messenger god, to meet Pluto. Mercury was skilled at bargaining, and Jupiter reasoned if anyone could get Pluto to change his mind, it would be Mercury.

Pluto and Mercury met, and it soon became clear that Pluto had no intention of letting Persephone return to Earth. On hearing that, Mercury had to think quickly. He suggested, "What if Persephone spends one month here in the underworld with you for every seed she ate and the rest of the time on Earth? Six seeds equals six months."

Pluto agreed. Every spring, Persephone returns to Earth, and her mother is overjoyed. So every spring, Ceres makes sure that nature looks its best to welcome Persephone back to Earth after her six dark months in the underworld. Because the fields flourish during the summer, there is food during the winter, when Persephone is in the underworld.

The World of CERES AND PERSEPHONE

Farming was the heart of the Roman Empire. Without a successful harvest, it was impossible to feed Rome's huge army and the rest of the Roman population.

FARMING

In fertile valleys north and south of Rome, farmers grew such cereal crops as wheat, rye, and barley. The cereal grains were *milled* (ground) to make flour, which bakers turned into bread and pastries. Poor people often ate pulse, a porridge made from leftover cereal grains. Olive trees and grape vines flourished on rockier hillsides. The olives were eaten as well as pressed and crushed to make olive oil, which was used in cooking. Grapes were turned into wine. Shepherds grazed sheep and goats, and other farmers raised hogs, cattle, and poultry.

Persephone (puhr SEHF uh nee) is seized by Pluto (PLOO toh), the lord of the underworld, in a painting from 1877.

A boy herds geese, in an ancient Roman mosaic.

The old boatman Charon (KAR uhn) ferries the *shade* (soul) of a dead person across the gloomy River Styx (stihks), in a painting from the early 1500's. The river marked the border between the world of the living and Hades (HAY deez), the land of the dead, in Roman and Greek mythology. Mercury, the messenger of the gods, guided the shades to the river. A ferocious, three-headed watchdog named Cerberus (SUR buhr uhs) guarded the entrance to Hades to make sure that no shades escaped back to the world of the living.

Different worlds existed in Hades. The souls of people who deserved neither punishment nor reward lived on a featureless plain. The souls of those who had led virtuous lives dwelled happily in Elysium (ih LIHZ ee uhm). The souls of those who had sinned greatly went to Tartarus (TAHR tuhr uhs), a pit far below Earth's surface. There they suffered eternal pain.

Worshipers of the goddess Ceres (SIHR eez) celebrate during a festival called the Cerealia (SIHR ee lee uh), in a tapestry from the 1700's. The festival was held each year from April 12 to April 19. According to legend, a temple to Ceres was built in Rome in 493 B.C., after she saved the city from a famine. The word *cereal* comes from her name.

DIANA AND ACTAEON

It was hardly Actaeon's fault that he stumbled upon the goddess Diana while she was bathing—but he suffered a terrible punishment all the same.

One day, Diana, the goddess of the hunt, was bathing with the nymphs (nihmfs) who so gracefully attended her in a secret grotto deep in a forest of pines and cypresses. Diana liked to bathe in the cave's clear, clean water after a day's hunting.

Unknown to Diana, Actaeon (ak TEE uhn), the son of King Cadmus (KAD muhs), had been hunting with friends close by that day. Also weary, Actaeon proposed to his friends that they all stop and rest. As his friends lay in the cool shade of the trees,

Actaeon decided to walk through the forest. He wandered for a while until he came upon the entrance to the grotto where Diana and her nymphs were bathing. Intrigued by the beauty of the spot, he looked in. The nymphs, spotting a man, screamed and rushed to Diana to protect her from Actaeon's gaze. But Diana was taller than her maidens, and they could not completely conceal her naked body from Actaeon's view.

Blushing at the sight of Actaeon, Diana looked around for her arrows, but they were not close to hand. Desperate, she threw some of the clear, pure water

from the grotto over the young man, saying, "Now go and tell everyone that you have seen Diana naked."

Actaeon did not have a chance to respond. As soon as the water touched him, his body started to change. Horns grew from the top of his head; his ears became pointed; and his hands turned into feet. His arms became long legs, and his body was soon covered in a hairy hide. He had become a stag.

Shocked, Actaeon, now huge and awkward, fled from the grotto, tears streaming from his eyes. "What do I do? Do I return to my palace or stay in the woods?" he thought to himself. As he hesitated, his dogs spotted him. They did not see Actaeon, the prince;

they saw a stag, which they wanted to chase. Soon they were racing after Actaeon, who leapt through the forest as fast as his four long stag legs would carry him.

He wanted to cry out, "I am your master," but no words came to him. Soon the dogs had caught him. They tore the flesh from his body, encouraged by Actaeon's friends and fellow hunters, who had no idea that the dogs were killing their friend. Instead, they called out to Actaeon to come and watch because he was missing the kill. Actaeon knew exactly what was happening, but there was nothing he could do to stop the dogs. At last, he died. Only then was Diana satisfied.

The World of
DIANA and ACTAEON

For the Romans, the story of the terrible death of Actaeon (ak TEE uhn) was a reminder of the punishments that await mortals who sin against the divinities.

DIANA

Diana was the daughter of Jupiter (JOO puh tuhr), the king of the gods, and the goddess Latona (luh TOH nuh) and the twin sister of the god Apollo (uh POL oh). Because she resembled the Greek goddess Artemis (AHR tuh mihs), Diana became associated with Artemis's myths and characteristics. Diana was a moon goddess and the goddess of young living things, particularly young animals, and of hunting. Artists often showed Diana wearing hunting clothes and carrying a bow and a quiver of arrows. She is usually accompanied by forest creatures and hunting dogs.

Nymphs (nihmfs), beautiful nature goddesses, often appear in Roman myths. Most nymphs served a god or goddess or a nymph of a higher rank. The Romans believed that nymphs were the daughters of Jupiter. Most nymphs lived in caves or trees near springs or rivers. Although they were goddesses, they were not immortal. Nymphs were sometimes shy. They were often friendly and kind to mortals but occasionally punished people who offended them.

Diana teases Cupid (KYOO pihd), the Roman god of love, in a painting from the 1700's. A person shot with one of Cupid's gold-tipped arrows supposedly was caused to fall in love by the wound.

Roman men hunt a wild boar and *stags* (male deer), in a mosaic from an ancient Roman *villa* (house). Wild beasts, including buffalo, wild boar, wolf, and deer, roamed the mountainsides and vast forests outside Rome. Hunting was a means of controlling the numbers of these animals as well as providing meat for people to eat. Hunting was also a popular, if dangerous, sport. Bears and boars could easily kill hunters, who prayed to Diana to keep them safe.

APOLLO AND DAPHNE

The Romans saw love as a powerful force acting on humans and gods alike. But as Apollo discovered, even gods could be unlucky in love.

Apollo (uh POL oh) was the god of prophecy as well as the god of archery, music, and light. Although a powerful god, he was unlucky in love. His first love was the beautiful water nymph Daphne (DAF nee), the daughter of the river god Peneus (puh NEE uhs). But Daphne wanted nothing to do with Apollo.

Apollo's devotion to Daphne and her coldness toward Apollo were both caused by Cupid (KYOO pihd), the god of love. Apollo had angered Cupid by

telling silly jokes. To get his revenge, Cupid fired a golden arrow at Apollo to make him fall in love. Then he fired a lead arrow at Daphne to make her reject Apollo.

But Apollo would not give up so easily. He refused to believe that Daphne would not, one day, fall in love with him. He chased the nymph through the woods, telling her how much he loved her. Still Daphne refused him, fleeing faster than the wind.

Apollo called out, "Stay, daughter of Peneus. I am not your enemy. I love you. Please do not rush away from me; I am worried you will fall and hurt yourself and it will be my fault. I only wish you well. I am the son of Jupiter and I know all things, past and present. My arrows fly true but an arrow has pierced my heart. I am the god of medicine but I know no cure for the illness that afflicts my heart."

Daphne did not slow down, barely catching what he said as she fled in terror. Apollo was angry and speeded up until he had almost caught her. Just as he reached out to grab Daphne, she called to Peneus to save her, "Help me, Father! Open up the earth or change my form so that I can escape this danger."

Barely had she spoken the words than her limbs went stiff, and her skin turned into bark. Her hair became leaves, her arms became branches, and her feet became stuck firmly in the ground. Her face became the top of a laurel tree, still just as beautiful as when she had been a water nymph.

Apollo could not believe it—his beautiful Daphne was now a laurel tree. He stroked the tree and kissed and talked to it, "Since you cannot be my wife, you will be my tree. I will wear a crown of your leaves so that you are always with me. Your leaves will always stay green and will never decay."

The nymph, who had spurned Apollo in life, now recognized his kindness and bowed her head in gratitude. From that day on, Apollo always wore a crown of laurel leaves, which were sacred to him.

The World of
APOLLO AND DAPHNE

Apollo (uh POL oh) was one of the gods the Romans believed was most closely involved in human lives. This story portrays him as being emotional and stubborn but ultimately kind and considerate.

THE ORACLE

The ancient Romans, like the ancient Greeks, believed that some prophets or prophetesses, called oracles (AWR uh kuhlz), had special powers to reveal the will of the gods and to foretell the future. The word *oracle* also referred to a shrine where people came to seek advice from these prophets or prophetesses. Most oracles were dedicated to Apollo. People who can tell the future appear in the myths of many cultures.

The Greek god Apollo (above) kept his name after joining the *pantheon* (collection) of Roman gods. In ancient Greece, Apollo was the god of the sun as well as of archery, healing, music, poetry, prophecy, and seafaring. The Romans worshiped Apollo chiefly as a god of healing and prophecy. He was always shown in sculptures as the ideal of manliness. But although attractive, poor Apollo was unlucky in love. He never married and was rejected by a number of women.

The oracle of Delphi (DEHL fy) (above), which was dedicated to the god Apollo, was the oldest and most influential religious shrine in ancient Greece and Rome. The town of Delphi lay on the southern slopes of Mount Parnassus in central Greece. According to legend, Apollo killed a large snake, the Python, in Delphi and learned the art of prophecy there. At a temple dedicated to Apollo, a priestess, often known as the Pythia (PIHTH ee uh), uttered strange and puzzling sounds while in a frenzy (right) believed to be inspired by the god. Temple priests interpreted these sounds to the public.

The laurel, a group of trees and shrubs, was considered sacred to Apollo. In paintings and sculptures, Apollo is usually shown wearing a wreath made from laurel leaves. At athletic games held in ancient Delphi, a city in Greece, winners were crowned with laurel wreaths. The Romans learned of this practice and adopted it to honor military commanders who had won their battles. Roman emperors later adopted the laurel wreath as a sign of divinity—that the emperor was the human form of a god. But the "leaves" in the emperors' wreaths were made of solid gold.

43

VULCAN, MARS, AND VENUS

The blacksmith god Vulcan was lame, but that did not prevent him getting his revenge on his wife, Venus, and Mars, the god of war.

Venus (VEE nuhs), the goddess of love, was the wife of Vulcan (VUHL kuhn), the lame, ugly son of the god Jupiter (JOO puh tuhr) and his wife, the goddess Juno (JOO noh). Vulcan was the god of fire and blacksmiths. He was also an architect, chariot builder, and armorer as well as the chief builder of the gods' dwellings. Everyone knew that Venus made love to both other gods and even mortal men. Vulcan knew this, too, and was often angry and jealous.

One day, another god came to see Vulcan. He told him that he had seen Venus together with Mars, the god of war, in Vulcan's palace.

Of course, Vulcan became furious. He stormed into his workshop and set to work making a huge metal net. The net was extremely light and fine. But it was so strong that it was impossible to break. Vulcan suspended the net from the rafters in the ceiling of his and Venus's bedroom. Then he tied each end of the net to the corners of the bed. The net was like a huge, invisible cobweb—the threads of metal were so thin that not even a god could see them. Then Vulcan pretended that he had been called away from the palace on business and left.

Venus came home soon after her husband had gone. Before long, Mars arrived, took Venus by the hand, and led her to the bed. As soon as they lay down, the finely woven web ensnared them in a tight grip. No

matter how hard they struggled, they could not escape from it. Suddenly, Vulcan returned, telling his servants that he had changed his mind about his trip. Frightened, the servants told Vulcan what had happened in his bedroom.

Screaming with rage, Vulcan called upon the gods, "Come and see this outrageous sight. Venus has never been faithful to me because I am lame." Vulcan insisted that he would not release the unfortunate lovers until Jupiter, Venus's father, had repaid the money Vulcan had given him so he could marry his daughter.

Neptune (NEHP toon), the god of the sea; Mercury (MUR kyuhr ee), the messenger of the gods; and Apollo (uh POL oh), the sun god, came to see the spectacle. They roared with laughter as Mars and Venus struggled under the net. "See how the lame Vulcan has tamed Mars, the fiercest of all the gods," they said, mocking the lovers.

Neptune offered to settle Jupiter's debt to Vulcan, and Vulcan reluctantly agreed. He lifted the net and set Venus and Mars free, and they fled as fast as they could.

The World of VULCAN, MARS, AND VENUS

The Roman gods often acted much like humans. They fell in love, cheated, squabbled, and tried to get revenge on one another.

Mars (below) was an important god to the Romans. He was the god of warfare as well as the father of the founders of Rome, Romulus (ROM yuh luhs) and Remus (REE muhs). The Romans believed that Mars helped them in their many military victories. The Emperor Augustus (63 B.C.–A.D. 41) built a temple to Mars in Rome, calling it the Temple of Mars the Avenger. Augustus believed that Mars had helped him to avenge the assassination of his adoptive father, the Emperor Julius Caesar (100–44 B.C.).

Vulcan (above, left) forges chains for Prometheus (proh MEE thee uhs), who was punished by the gods for stealing fire to give to humans.

VULCAN

Vulcan was the only Roman god with a physical disability. He was unfortunate because his wife, Venus, was more attracted to his half-brother, Mars, than she was to him. But Vulcan was a useful god, as Roman blacksmiths were vital for equipping the empire's army. In Roman mythology, Vulcan was originally the god of fire, especially destructive fire. But he became identified with Hephaestus (hih FEHS tuhs), the Greek god of metal-working.

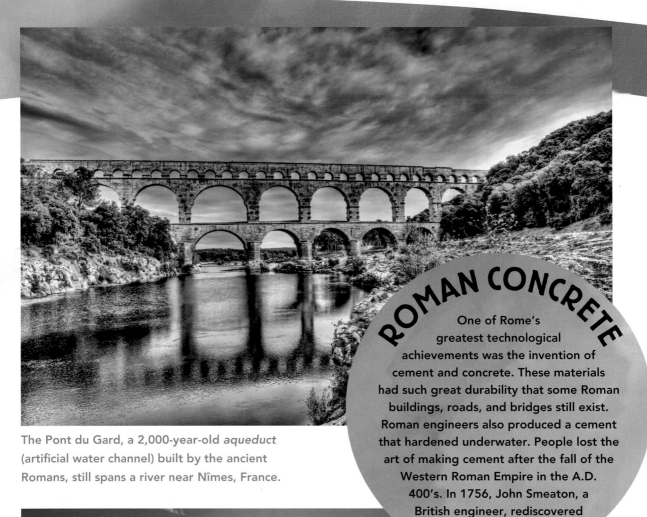

The Pont du Gard, a 2,000-year-old *aqueduct* (artificial water channel) built by the ancient Romans, still spans a river near Nîmes, France.

ROMAN CONCRETE

One of Rome's greatest technological achievements was the invention of cement and concrete. These materials had such great durability that some Roman buildings, roads, and bridges still exist. Roman engineers also produced a cement that hardened underwater. People lost the art of making cement after the fall of the Western Roman Empire in the A.D. 400's. In 1756, John Smeaton, a British engineer, rediscovered how to make cement.

An ancient road paved with stones in Spain is one of many examples of Roman engineering that has survived to modern times. Roman roads were well constructed and remarkably straight. Military forces were able to move along them quickly. After the army had *pacified* (calmed) a newly conquered region, Roman administrators used the roads to promote trade and communication.

49

ECHO AND NARCISSUS

Echo and Narcissus were two of the most tragic characters in Roman mythology. They each suffered a terrible fate.

Echo (EHK oh), a beautiful nymph (nihmf) who lived in the forest, had one big failing—she never stopped talking. One day, Juno (JOO noh), the queen of the gods, came to the forest. She suspected that her husband, Jupiter (JOO puh tuhr), was there, flirting with nymphs.

Juno was right, but Echo talked and talked to her, giving the nymphs and Jupiter time to escape. Juno was furious. To punish Echo, she told her "From now on, you will never say the first word. You will only have the last word, of which you are so fond."

Now, Echo was in love with a beautiful youth called Narcissus (nahr SIHS uhs). She watched him when he visited the forest. She wanted to talk to him, but because of Juno's curse, Narcissus had to speak first. At last, one day, he felt that Echo was close by and watching him, and he spoke, "Who's here?"

"Here," replied Echo, because that is all she could say. Echo threw herself on Narcissus, but he cruelly rejected her. "I would rather die than become your partner," he said. Heartbroken, Echo hid herself away in a cave.

One day sometime later, while out hunting, Narcissus came across a pool of crystal-clear water in the forest. He was thirsty and exhausted and stooped down to have a drink. To his amazement, he saw a beautiful face in the water. Not

realizing that the face was his own, he fell in love with the reflection. Narcissus first tried to kiss the face, and then plunged his hand into the water to touch it. But the face fled at his touch, returning only when the water became smooth again and Narcissus moved close to it.

Narcissus could not understand why the beautiful face did not return his affection. He couldn't think of anything other than the face that he pined for. Soon he was wasting away because he was not eating, and the nymphs mocked him. Echo, however, still loved him, and when he cried "Alas" at his beautiful face, she answered the same, calling "Alas."

Finally, one day, only a perfumed, bright white flower with slender green leaves remained where Narcissus had gazed at his beautiful face. That flower still bears his name today. Grief-stricken, Echo also wasted away until there was nothing left of her but her voice, which still could reply only by repeating the last word that anyone called out to her.

The World of OVID

The tale of Echo (EHK oh) and Narcissus (nahr SIHS uhs) appears in the *Metamorphoses* (MEHT uh MAWR fuh seez), a 15-volume collection of stories in verse by the Roman poet Ovid (OV ihd). The *Metamorphoses* describes the adventures and love affairs of deities and heroes, with more than 200 tales taken from Greek and Roman legends and myths. *Metamorphoses* means *transformation,* or change, in Latin, and the book deals with many kinds of transformation. Ovid's stories are filled with characters from ancient history, legend, and other sources that were familiar to the ancient Romans. Many of the stories remain popular today.

MASTER STORYTELLER

Ovid (43 B.C.-A.D. 17?), was a great Roman poet who is most famous for his witty and sophisticated love poems. Ovid, however, thought the *Metamorphoses* was his greatest work. In A.D. 8, Emperor Augustus banished Ovid to an isolated fishing village on the Black Sea. He was angry at Ovid for writing a guide to *adultery* (unfaithfulness by a husband or wife). Ovid wrote many poems pleading to return to Rome. But his pleas were ignored, and he died in exile.

Orpheus (AWR fee uhs) was a superb musician. After his wife, Eurydice (yoo RIHD ih see), died on their wedding day, Orpheus traveled to the underworld to bring her back. The rulers of the underworld agreed to release Eurydice if Orpheus did not look at her until they reached the upper world. But at the last minute, Orpheus turned to see his wife, who was forced back to the land of the dead.

One of Ovid's myths tells of a princess named Europa (yu ROH puh) who enchanted Zeus with her beauty. The king of the gods disguised himself as a handsome white bull and tempted the princess to climb on his back. Zeus then swam to the island of Crete. The continent of Europe is named for the princess who never returned home.

Icarus (IHK uhr uhs) was the young son of Daedalus (DEHD uh luhs), a skilled inventor. Ovid told how Daedalus lived for a time on Crete, where he made many inventions for King Minos (MY nuhs). Among these was the Labyrinth, a mazelike building that imprisoned a monster called the Minotaur (MIHN uh tawr). However, Daedalus angered Minos by helping the Greek hero who killed the Minotaur. As punishment, the king locked Daedalus and Icarus in the Labyrinth. To escape, Daedalus made two pairs of wings from feathers, wax, and thread. Daedalus cautioned Icarus not to fly too close to the sun because the heat would melt the wax. But Icarus found flying thrilling and, ignoring his father's warning, he soared higher and higher. Soon Icarus's wings fell apart, and he plunged to his death in the sea.

The story of bloody battle between the centaurs (SEHN tawrs) and a people called the Lapiths also appears in the *Metamorphoses*. Centaurs were creatures with the upper body of a man and the lower body of a horse. Unfortunately, they had a terrible reputation because they often behaved barbarically. At the wedding feast of the daughter of the king of the Lapiths, the centaurs became drunk and tried to kidnap the Lapith women. The leader of the centaurs even tried to kidnap the bride. A fierce battle followed. Although the Lapiths defeated the centaurs, there were many deaths on both sides.

CUPID AND PSYCHE

No one expected Cupid, the god of love, to fall in love himself—until he met the beautiful Psyche.

Psyche (SY kee) was the youngest of three sisters and, by far, the most beautiful. Many admirers considered her more beautiful than Venus (VEE nuhs), the goddess of love and beauty. When Venus discovered that Psyche's beauty was prized above her own, she became furious. She sent her son Cupid (KYOO bihd), the god of love, to punish Psyche by giving her a potion that would prevent anyone from falling in love with her. But while Cupid was administering the potion, he fell madly in love with Psyche himself.

Psyche's two older sisters soon found husbands, but no one wanted to marry Psyche. Her parents worried that they had somehow offended the gods and consulted the oracle (AWR uh kuhl) of Apollo to ask for guidance. Apollo told them that no man would marry Psyche. But, he said, her future husband—an ugly monster—was waiting for her on the top of a nearby mountain. So Psyche agreed to marry the monster and climbed to the mountaintop.

When Psyche arrived, she was amazed. She found a fabulous palace, filled with treasures. While she gazed, awestruck, at its golden pillars and beautifully painted ceilings, an unknown voice addressed her, "Queen, all that you see is yours. We are here to serve your every need." Then Psyche enjoyed the most delicious dinner and listened to soothing music played by invisible performers. But she had still not met her future husband.

Finally at night, Psyche's husband arrived. But, to her surprise, he left before sunrise. On the second day of their marriage, Psyche's husband once again arrived at night and fled before any light filled the sky. And that became the pattern of their life together.

When Psyche and her husband were together, he was kind and attentive,

and Psyche was happy. She begged him to stay with her all day, but he refused. "Why do you need to see me?" he asked. "Aren't you sure of my love for you?"

Psyche was content until one day her sisters came to visit. Seeing the

splendor in which Psyche lived, they were filled with jealousy. When Psyche told them she saw her husband only at night, they insisted, "You will never be truly happy until you see your husband."

After they left, Psyche carried on as before, but her sisters' words troubled her. Finally she could resist their warning no longer, and she hid a lamp in her bedroom. After her husband fell asleep, she shined a light on him. To her astonishment, she saw that he was not a monster but an extremely handsome man. Her husband was Cupid. To punish Psyche for doubting his love, Cupid disappeared.

Realizing her stupidity, Psyche wandered day and night to find her husband, but it was useless. Finally, out of desperation, she consulted Cupid's mother, Venus. Venus, still angry about Psyche's beauty, set Psyche three seemingly impossible challenges as the price for her help. But Psyche accomplished all three of them.

When Cupid found out what his mother had done, he persuaded Jupiter (JOO puh tuhr) to stop Venus from tormenting Psyche. Jupiter also made Psyche immortal. So she and Cupid lived happily together for the rest of time along with their daughter, Voluptas (vol uhp tas), the goddess of pleasure.

The World of
CUPID AND PSYCHE

The story of Cupid (KYOO pihd) and Psyche (SY kee) lives on today, often retold in movies and books as a boy-meets-girl love story in which the lovers eventually overcome the challenges they encounter.

Cupid, the son of Venus (VEE nuhs) and Mars, was the Roman god of love. His equivalent in ancient Greece was Eros (IHR os). The earliest images of Cupid show him as a handsome, athletic young man. But by the mid-300's B.C., he was being depicted as a small, winged child who played tricks on gods and humans to make them fall passionately in love. He carried a golden quiver full of arrows made from gold and lead. A person shot with one of Cupid's gold-tipped arrows supposedly fell in love. His lead-tipped arrows had the opposite effect.

The planet Venus is the brightest object in Earth's sky apart from the sun and moon. For this reason, the ancient Romans named the planet for their goddess of beauty. Venus is so bright because it is surrounded by thick clouds of sulfuric acid that reflect about 70 percent of the sunlight that strikes the planet.

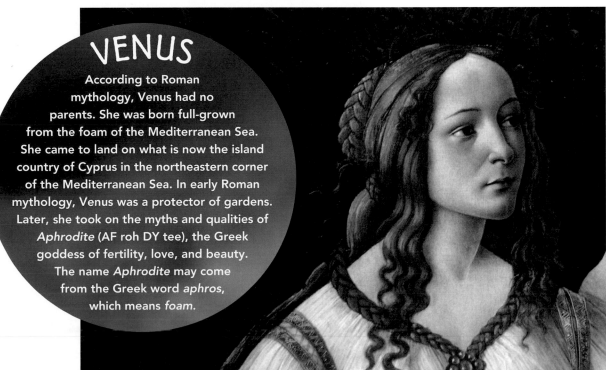

VENUS

According to Roman mythology, Venus had no parents. She was born full-grown from the foam of the Mediterranean Sea. She came to land on what is now the island country of Cyprus in the northeastern corner of the Mediterranean Sea. In early Roman mythology, Venus was a protector of gardens. Later, she took on the myths and qualities of *Aphrodite* (AF roh DY tee), the Greek goddess of fertility, love, and beauty. The name *Aphrodite* may come from the Greek word *aphros*, which means *foam*.

DEITIES OF ANCIENT ROME

Apollo (uh POL oh)

Apollo had many roles in the Roman *pantheon* (collection of gods), including being the god of light, the sun, truth, and music. The Romans borrowed Apollo directly from the Greeks, which is why he has the same name in Greek and Latin. Although handsome, Apollo was unlucky with goddesses and human women.

Ceres (SIHR eez)

The goddess of grain, Ceres was the mother of Persephone, who was stolen away to the underworld by Pluto. For the six months of the year that Persephone spent with Pluto, Ceres mourned her daughter and plants ceased growing; when Ceres rejoiced at her daughter's return, she caused spring to begin.

Cupid (KYOO pihd)

The god of love and desire, Cupid was Venus's son. He was portrayed as a cherubic little boy with a bow with which to shoot arrows of love into the hearts of mortals.

Diana (dy AN uh)

Goddess of the hunt and wild animals, Diana and her companion nymphs all swore never to marry and to remain devoted to the hunt; she was also a goddess of childbirth and the moon.

Hades (HAY deez)

In Greek mythology, Hades ruled the kingdom of the dead, which had the same name. The ancient Romans preserved without change almost all the myths about Hades and his kingdom, but they called the god Pluto.

Janus (JAY nuhs)

The god of change, Janus had one face looking forward to the future and one looking into the past. The month of January was named for him, as one of his chief responsibilities is turning the old year into a new one at the end of every December.

Juno (JOO noh)

Jupiter's wife, Juno, was the queen of heaven and goddess of marriage. The month of June was sacred to her and was thought by Romans to be the best time to hold weddings. Like her Greek counterpart, Hera, the wife of Zeus, Juno was always on the look out for the wrongdoings of her husband Jupiter.

Jupiter (JOO puh tuhr)

King of heaven and god of thunder, Jupiter (also known as Jove) was the special protector of Rome. He was given the title "Optimus Maximus"—best and greatest. Jupiter figured widely in Roman myths for chasing nymphs and mortal women, and his troublemaking.

Latona (luh TOH nuh)

Goddess of motherhood and modesty, Latona was the mother of Apollo and Diana.

Mars (mahrz)

The god of war, Mars was also the father of Romulus and Remus, the legendary founders of Rome. Bearded and fierce, he was also the god of farming and was worshiped particularly by Roman farmers.

Mercury (MUR kyuhr ee)

Often shown wearing a winged cap and winged sandals, Mercury was the messenger of the gods. More importantly, Mercury was the god of merchandise and business.

Neptune (NEHP toon)

An all-conquering and powerful sea god, Neptune was the triton-wielding cause of storms. He was feared by sailors, who prayed to him for good weather before setting out on voyages.

Persephone (puhr SEHF uh nee)

Daughter of Ceres, Persephone became Pluto's wife after he fell in love with her beauty. She lived for half the year with Pluto in the underworld, and the other half with her mother; her return caused the season of spring to begin again on Earth.

Pluto (PLOO toh)

Pluto was king of the Roman underworld, where he was the judge of the dead, deciding which of the dead souls would suffer in Tartarus and which would live happily in Elysium.

Psyche (SY kee)

The beautiful Psyche was born a mortal but became a goddess after her marriage to Cupid; the goddess Venus became jealous of Psyche because some people thought she was more beautiful than Venus.

Quirinus (kwih RY nuhs)

Quirinus was the god of the common Roman people. He was believed to promote the general prosperity and welfare of the community. Over time, Romans came to believe that Quirinus was the divine *incarnation* (form) of Romulus, one of the mythical cofounders of Rome. After about 200 B.C., Quirinus lost much of his importance to the Romans.

Venus (VEE nuhs)

Venus was goddess of love and beauty. The planet Venus is the only planet named after a female goddess.

Vesta (VEHS tuh)

Vesta was the goddess of the hearth and the figurehead of the Vestal Virgins. These priestesses dedicated themselves to the worship of Vesta, vowing to remain untouched by men for 30 years.

Voluptas (vol uhp tas)

The daughter of Cupid and Psyche, Voluptas was the Roman goddess of pleasure.

Vulcan (VUHL kuhn)

The Roman god of metalworking, Vulcan was a lame god married to the unfaithful Venus. Vulcan was similar to the god of metalworking and the forge of the Etruscans, an ancient people who lived on what is now the Italian peninsula before the Romans.

GLOSSARY

assassination A murder carried out because of the victim's political beliefs or position.

avenge To inflict harm on someone in return for an injury or a wrong done.

centaur A creature in Greek mythology with the upper body of a man and the lower body of a horse.

divinity A divine being; a god or goddess.

forum The public square or marketplace of a Roman town.

grotto A small cave, often artificial or constructed by humans.

hearth The area immediately around a fireplace.

heirs People who inherit the property of a predecessor, particularly a parent.

immortality The quality of being able to live forever.

lyre An ancient stringed musical instrument that resembles a small harp. It has a bowl- or box-shaped frame with two arms extending upward. A crossbar is attached to the top of the arms.

myth A traditional story that a people tell to explain their own origins or the origins of natural and social phenomena. Myths often involve gods, spirits, and other supernatural beings.

nymphs Spirits of nature who appear as beautiful young women and live in rivers, woods, and other natural locations.

oath A solemn promise about one's future actions or behavior.

oracle A priest or priestess through whom gods and goddesses pass advice and prophecies to humans.

pantheon A collection of all the gods and goddesses of a religion. The Pantheon was also a temple in Rome dedicated to all the Roman deities.

prophecy A prediction of something that will happen in the future.

ritual A solemn religious ceremony in which a set of actions are performed in a specific order.

sacred Something that is connected with the gods or goddesses and so should be treated with respectful worship.

seduced Attracted into doing something that is not sensible.

shade A ghost or spirit; the soul of a dead person.

supernatural Describes something that cannot be explained by science or by the laws of nature, which is, therefore, said to be caused by beings such as gods, spirits, or ghosts.

thunderbolt A shaft or bolt that is the destructive part of a flash of lightning, believed to be thrown by a god such as Jupiter.

Vestal Virgin A priestess who kept the sacred fire burning on the altar of the temple of the goddess Vesta in Rome and who vowed to remain unmarried for 30 years.

villa A house built for wealthy Romans in the country or along the seashore.

FOR FURTHER INFORMATION

Books

Allan, Tony. *Exploring the Life, Myth, and Art of Ancient Rome* (Civilizations of the World). Rosen Publishing Group, 2012.

Allan, Tony, and Sara Maitland. *Ancient Greece and Rome: Myths and Beliefs* (World Mythologies). Rosen Publishing Group, 2012.

Daly, Kathleen N., and Marian Rengel. *Greek and Roman Mythology A to Z* (Mythology A to Z). Chelsea House Publications, 2009.

Day, Malcolm. *100 Characters from Classical Mythology: Discover the Fascinating Stories of the Greek and Roman Deities*. Barron's Educational, 2007.

Elgin, Kathy. *Roman Myths* (Myths from Many Lands). Windmill Books, 2009.

Hansen, William. *Handbook of Classical Mythology* (Handbooks of World Mythology). ABC–CLIO, 2004.

Hibbert, Clare. *Terrible Tales of Ancient Rome* (Monstrous Myths). Gareth Stevens Publishing, 2014.

Hunt, Jilly. *Roman Myths and Legends* (All About Myths). Capstone Raintree, 2013.

Johnson, Robin. *Understanding Roman Myths* (Myths Understood). Crabtree Publishing Company, 2012.

Lunge-Larsen, Lise. *Gifts from the Gods: Ancient Words and Wisdom from Greek and Roman Mythology*. Houghton Mifflin Books for Children, 2011.

National Geographic Essential Visual History of World Mythology. National Geographic Society, 2008.

Philip, Neil. *Eyewitness Mythology* (DK Eyewitness Books). DK Publishing, 2011.

Roman, Luke, and Monica Roman. *Encyclopedia of Greek and Roman Mythology* (Facts on File Libary of Religion and Mythology). Facts on File, 2010.

Schomp, Virginia. *The Ancient Romans* (Myths of the World). Marshall Cavendish Benchmark, 2009.

Scurman, Ike, and John Malam. *Ancient Roman Civilization* (Ancient Civilizations and their Myths and Legends). Rosen Publishing Group, 2010.

Websites

http://www.godchecker.com/pantheon/roman-mythology.php
A directory of Roman deities from God Checker, written in a light-hearted style but with accurate information.

http://www.pantheon.org/areas/mythology/europe/roman/
Encyclopedia Mythica page with links to many pages about Roman myths. Click on the link to "available articles."

http://www.mythome.org/roman.html
A page with links to articles about the different Roman gods.

http://www.crystalinks.com/rome.html
This Crystal Links page has links to pages about all aspects of ancient Rome, including its gods, goddesses, and myths.

http://www.bbc.co.uk/schools/primaryhistory/romans/religion
A BBC website about Roman religion.

INDEX

PRONUNCIATION KEY	
Sound	As in
a	hat, map
ah	father, far
ai	care, air
aw	order
aw	all
ay	age, face
ch	child, much
ee	equal, see
ee	machine, city
eh	let, best
ih	it, pin, hymn
k	coat, look
o	hot, rock
oh	open, go
oh	grow, tableau
oo	rule, move, food
ow	house, out
oy	oil, voice
s	say, nice
sh	she, abolition
u	full, put
u	wood
uh	cup, butter
uh	flood
uh	about, ameba
uh	taken, purple
uh	pencil
uh	lemon
uh	circus
uh	labyrinth
uh	curtain
uh	Egyptian
uh	section
uh	fabulous
ur	term, learn, sir, work
y	icon, ice, five
yoo	music
zh	pleasure